To:

From:

A Bit of Applause for Santa Claus

Published by Sourcebooks, Inc.
P.O. Box 4410, Naperville, Illinois 60567-4410
(630) 961-3900
FAX: (630) 961-2168
www.sourcebooks.com

ISBN 1-4022-0553-8

Printed and bound in China
SNP 10 9 8 7 6 5 4 3 2 1

A Bit of Applause for Santa Claus

Jeannie Schick-Jacobowitz ★ Susie Schick-Pierce ★ Muffin Drake ★ Shannon Drake ★ Illustrated by Wendy Wallin Malinow

SOURCEBOOKS, INC.
NAPERVILLE, ILLINOIS

This book is dedicated to

everyone who makes our holidays

and our lives magical:

Phil, Garrett, Richard,

Jimmy and Sebastian

(our own special Santas).

We applaud you!

'Twas the night after Christmas,
I paused to recall
How despite all the chaos,
we've laughed through it all.

The house was a mess,
there'd been so much to do.
No one else would put up
with this clutter but you.

"To-do" lists were long
with no clear end in sight,
You helped me stay focused
each day and each night.

No time for the gym,
no time for a run.
No long winter's nap,
too much work to be done!

Though visions of hot tubs
had danced in your head
You were shoveling snow,
working so hard instead!

You got so excited!
White Christmas with snow!
With the kids and the neighbors
a-sledding you go.

Your eyes–how they twinkle!
Your smiles never vary!
You're truly my hero
Because you're so merry!

You remind me to laugh
and to keep my good cheer;
That's especially important
at this time of year.

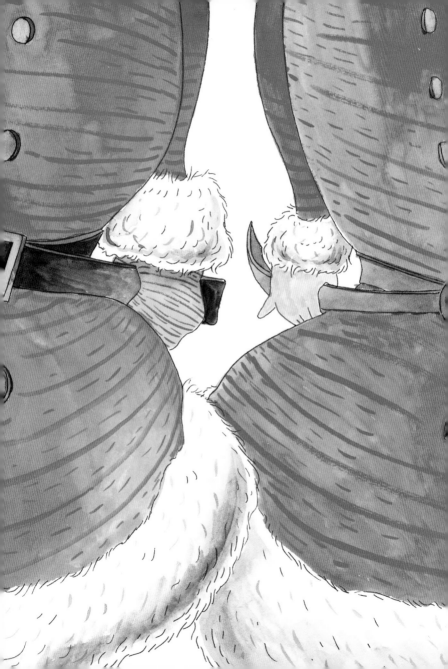

You remind me, "It's Christmas!
Don't worry, have fun!
We can tighten our belts
when it's over and done."

A wink of your eye
And you straighten me out.

You're the reason I don't have a reason to pout.

You hopped on your sleigh
for that last midnight run,
For without extra batteries
we'd have no fun!

Our own "elves" were snuggled
all safe in their beds,
While jingles from rap songs
played on in their heads.

I went to the window
for fresh air to breathe,
And saw you'd made time
to hang up my pine wreath.

I stood in amazement
and then turned around—
You had tidied the house
without making a sound.

The tree had been trimmed,
the computer shut down.
Every gift had been wrapped,
and with nary a frown!

As I took it all in
and saw love everywhere,
What a comfort it was
just to know you were there.

Then down in the kitchen
I heard something splatter,
I sprang to my feet
To see what was the matter.

Away down the hallway
I flew like a flash,
Tore open the door
and tripped over the trash.

As the moon lit your face
my heart started to glow.
You were sprinkled with flour
from your head to your toe.

You had baked us some cookies,
made eggnog to drink.
How they looked didn't matter:
You gave me that wink!

You were singing the carols,
I whistled the same,
And between us we called
all the reindeer by name.

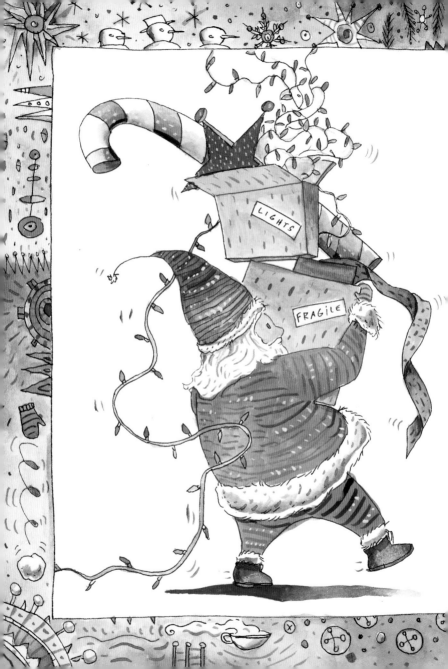

Holidays are so happy
with you in my life.
You help without question
and ease all the strife.

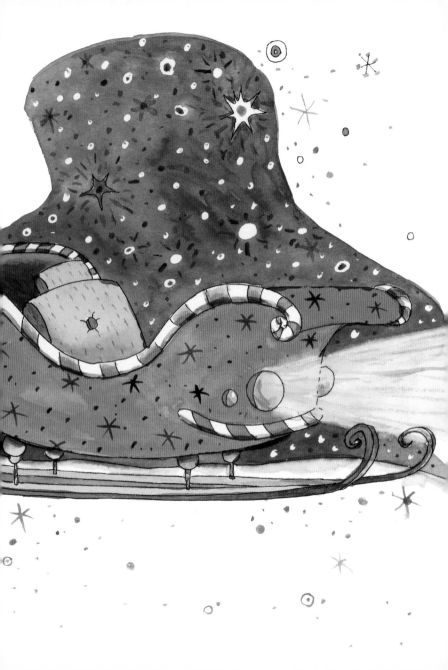

Merry Christmas to you
with your spirit so bright.
You've inspired my life
and are my guiding light.

The presents I love aren't found under the tree. It's your presence each day that means so much to me!

Your love and devotion
rate special applause,
So I give a big cheer
for my own Special Claus.